J

First
Facts®

REALLY **SCARY** STUFF

# SCARY STORIES

by Jim Whiting

**Consultant:**
Elizabeth Tucker
Professor of English
Binghamton University
Binghamton, New York

CAPSTONE PRESS
a capstone imprint

First Facts is published by Capstone Press,
1710 Roe Crest Drive, North Mankato, Minnesota 56003.
www.capstonepub.com

 Books published by Capstone Press are manufactured with paper
containing at least 10 percent post-consumer waste.

*Library of Congress Cataloging-in-Publication Data*
Whiting, Jim, 1951–
   Scary stories / by Jim Whiting.
   p. cm. — (First facts. Really scary stuff)
   Summary: "Describes legendary scary stories and explores whether or not the stories
could be true" — Provided by publisher.
   Includes bibliographical references and index.
   ISBN 978-1-4296-3969-9 (library binding : alk. paper)
   1. Ghosts — Juvenile literature. 2. Alien abduction — Juvenile literature. I. Title.
II. Series.
BF1461.W487 2010
133.1   dc22                               2009023965

**Editorial Credits**

Jennifer Besel, editor; Alison Thiele, designer; Marcie Spence, media researcher;
   Eric Manske, production specialist

**Photo Credits**

Alamy/Mary Evans Picture Library, 6, 8, 16; Alamy/Lordprice Collection, 14; The Bridgeman
Art Library/Private Collection, 20; The Bridgeman Art Library/Private Collection/Peter Newark
Historical Pictures, 21; Capstone Studio/Karon Dubke, 11; CORBIS/Bettmann, 15; Fortean Picture
Library, 12, 13, 18; iStockphoto/Elerium, 5; Shutterstock/Jean L F, cover

**The legends and stories presented in this book may have different versions. The versions used
in this book are considered by researchers to be the most common telling of the event or story.**

Printed in the United States of America in North Mankato, Minnesota.
122013
007882R

# TABLE OF CONTENTS

# TALES OF TERROR

Scary stories cover all kinds of topics. Some tell of headless pirates. Other tales explore space aliens on earth. But all scary stories have one thing in common — they are creepy! Get ready for six stories that will make your hair stand on end.

Scary stories may seem real, but are they?

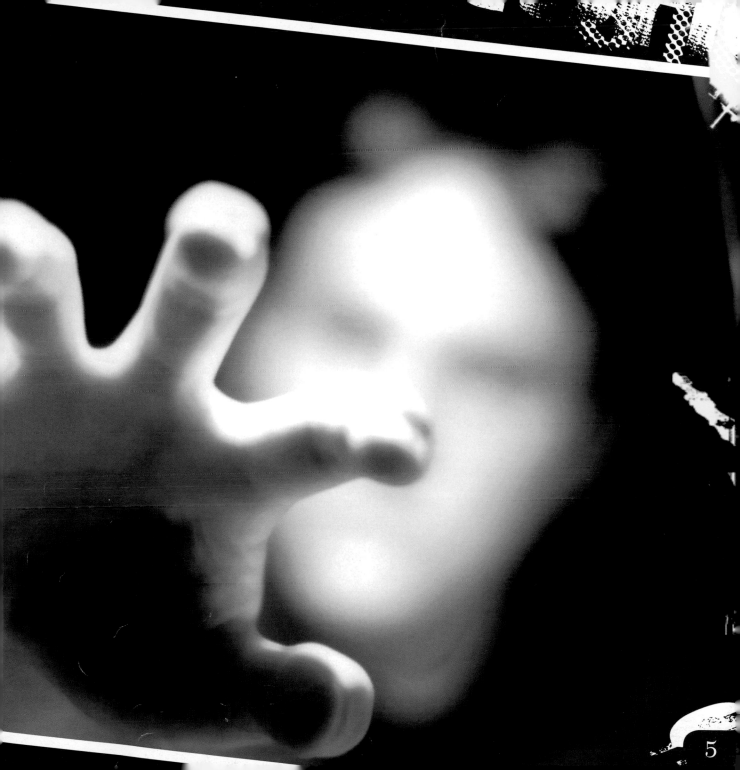

5

# AN ANGRY GHOST

It was 1878. Stories about a young woman named Esther Cox began in Amherst, Nova Scotia. The stories said a ghost wouldn't leave the young woman alone. The ghost made pans, potatoes, and pieces of plaster fly inside the house. The ghost wrote messages on the walls. It wrote, "Esther Cox! You are mine to kill."

Many ghost stories tell of objects flying through the air.

the Cox family home in Amherst, Nova Scotia

Stories said the ghost spoke to Esther and her family. The ghost said it would burn down the house. According to legend, the family even saw lit matches fall from the ceiling.

legend — an old story that could be believable

# FACT OR FICTION

## Was a Ghost Trying to Hurt Esther Cox?

**Yes** A doctor treated Esther in her home. He claimed he heard the ghost pounding and saw writing on the walls.

**No** A man put Esther on stage, saying people would see the ghost's activities. Nothing happened during the show.

**Yes** More than 12 people also claimed to see strange events in the house.

**No** Many of Esther's neighbors believed she made up the story. They never saw anything strange.

**Yes** When Esther left home, the strange events stopped. They started again when she returned.

**No** The events stopped after Esther got married. She never had problems in her other homes.

# HITCHING A RIDE

The story of the hitchhiker begins on a dark night. A man drives by a girl who is looking for a ride. He stops and offers to take her home. The girl agrees and gets in the car. When he arrives at her house, the girl is gone.

At the house, a woman says the girl is her dead daughter. The daughter's ghost hitches a ride every year on the **anniversary** of her death.

This story isn't true . . . or is it?

**anniversary** — a date that is remembered because something important happened

# MYSTERIOUS TOMB

The Chase family **tomb** in Barbados had been sealed shut for years. In 1812, workers opened the tomb. Inside, they found **coffins** thrown everywhere. But they saw no footprints in the sand around the coffins.

**tomb** — a room for holding a dead body
**coffin** — a container where a dead body is placed

the Chase family tomb

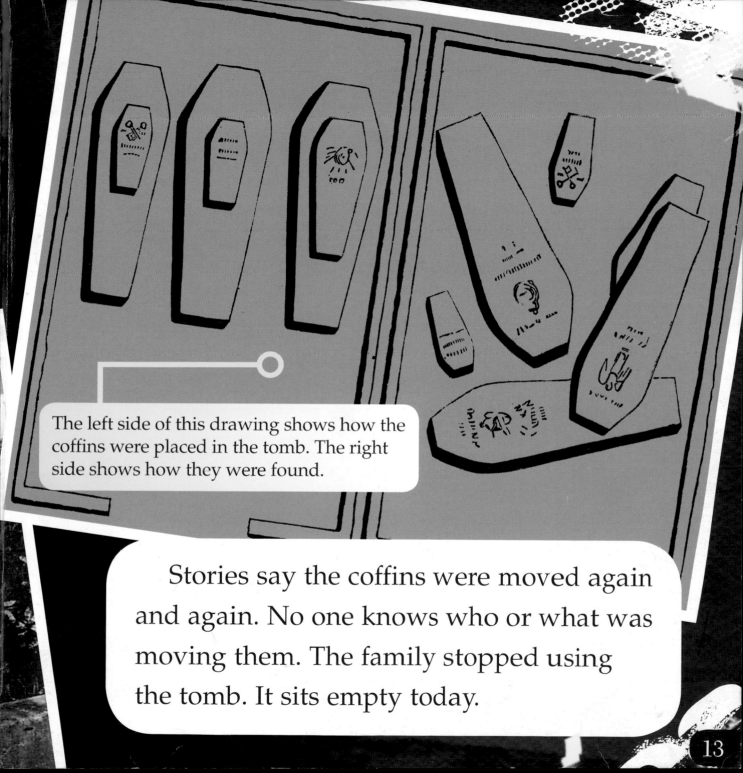

The left side of this drawing shows how the coffins were placed in the tomb. The right side shows how they were found.

Stories say the coffins were moved again and again. No one knows who or what was moving them. The family stopped using the tomb. It sits empty today.

# A BANK ROBBER'S GHOST

In the 1930s, John Dillinger was a famous bank robber. One night, Dillinger left a Chicago movie theater. FBI agents were waiting. They killed Dillinger in an alley near the theater.

John Dillinger

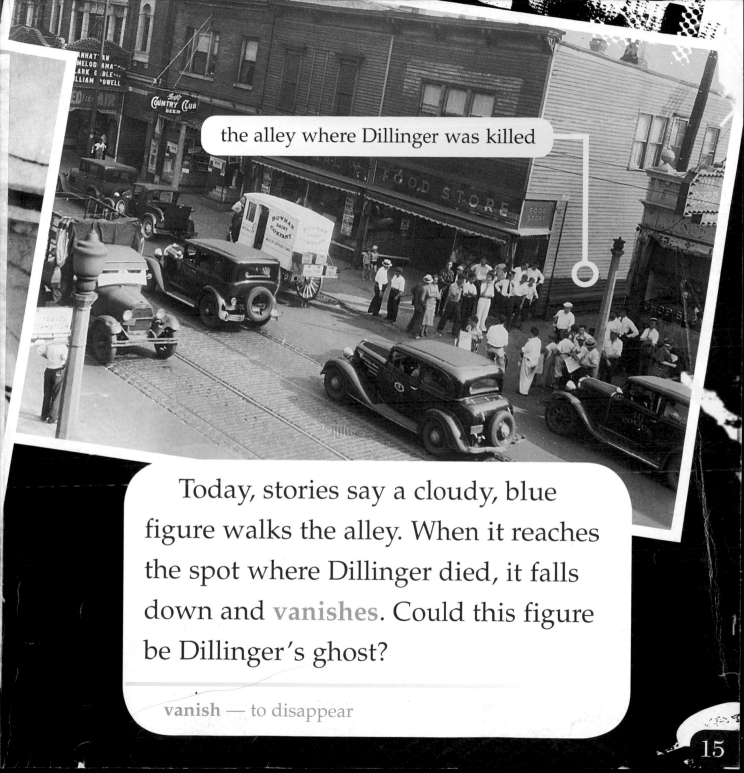

the alley where Dillinger was killed

Today, stories say a cloudy, blue figure walks the alley. When it reaches the spot where Dillinger died, it falls down and vanishes. Could this figure be Dillinger's ghost?

vanish — to disappear

# TAKEN BY ALIENS

Barney and Betty Hill's story about aliens is creepy. But is it true?

In 1961, the Hills were driving down a dark road. They spotted a bright light in the sky. The light sped toward them. The Hills soon realized it wasn't just a light. They saw a round spaceship with rows of windows. They said aliens looked out at them.

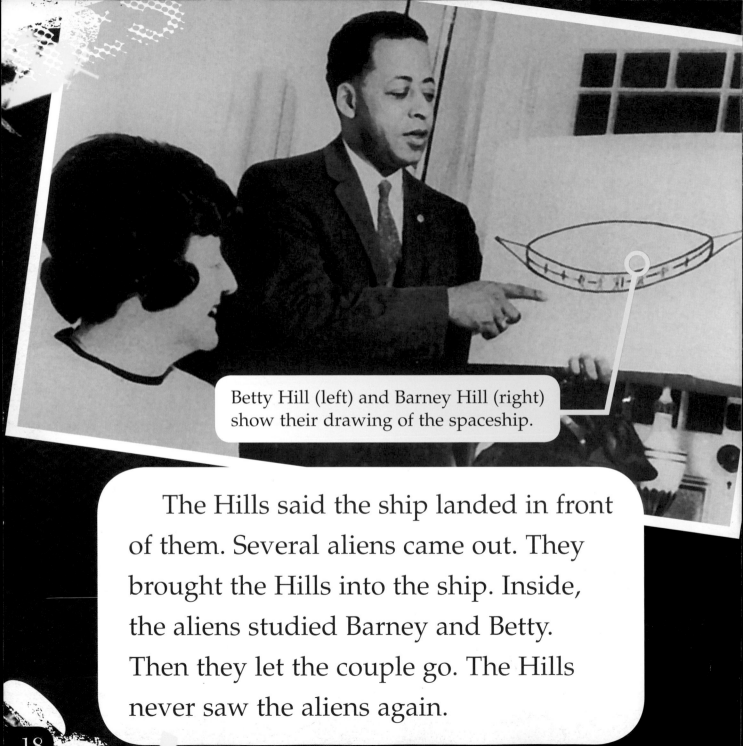

Betty Hill (left) and Barney Hill (right) show their drawing of the spaceship.

The Hills said the ship landed in front of them. Several aliens came out. They brought the Hills into the ship. Inside, the aliens studied Barney and Betty. Then they let the couple go. The Hills never saw the aliens again.

# FACT OR FICTION

## Were Barney and Betty Hill Studied by Aliens?

**Yes** Barney and Betty didn't tell their story for a long time. They feared people wouldn't believe it.

**Yes** Government officials were interested in the Hills' story. The officials wrote a report about the Hills' experience.

**Yes** Every year, thousands of other people report being taken by aliens.

**No** The Hills didn't know details about the aliens until a doctor hypnotized them. The story they remembered afterward might not be real.

**No** The Hills hired an author to write their story. They may have made up the story for fame or money.

**No** One of the Hills may have dreamed the event and told the other. Together they believed it happened.

hypnotize — to put someone into a trance

# HEADLESS PIRATE

Blackbeard was one of the most feared pirates. In 1718, English sailors fought this terrible pirate. They slashed off his head. They hung it on the ship for all to see.

Blackbeard

Stories say Blackbeard's headless body still floats off North Carolina's coast. Sometimes the body rises out of the water to search for its head.

Are any of these stories true? That's a question for you to answer.

# GLOSSARY

**anniversary** (an-uh-VUR-suh-ree) — a date that is remembered because something important happened on that day

**coffin** (KAWF-in) — a long container into which a dead body is placed

**hypnotize** (HIP-nuh-tize) — to put someone into a trance

**legend** (LEJ-uhnd) — a story handed down from earlier times that could seem believable

**tomb** (TOOM) — a grave, room, or building for holding a dead body

**vanish** (VAN-ish) — to disappear suddenly

# Read More

**Hamilton, Sue.** *Blackbeard.* Pirates. Edina, Minn.: Abdo, 2007.

**McCormick, Lisa Wade.** *Alien Abductions.* Mysteries of Science. Mankato, Minn.: Capstone Press, 2010.

**Walker, Kathryn.** *Mysteries of Alien Visitors and Abductions.* Unsolved! New York: Crabtree, 2009.

# Internet Sites

FactHound offers a safe, fun way to find Internet sites related to this book. All of the sites on FactHound have been researched by our staff.

Here's all you do:

Visit *www.facthound.com*

FactHound will fetch the best sites for you!

# INDEX